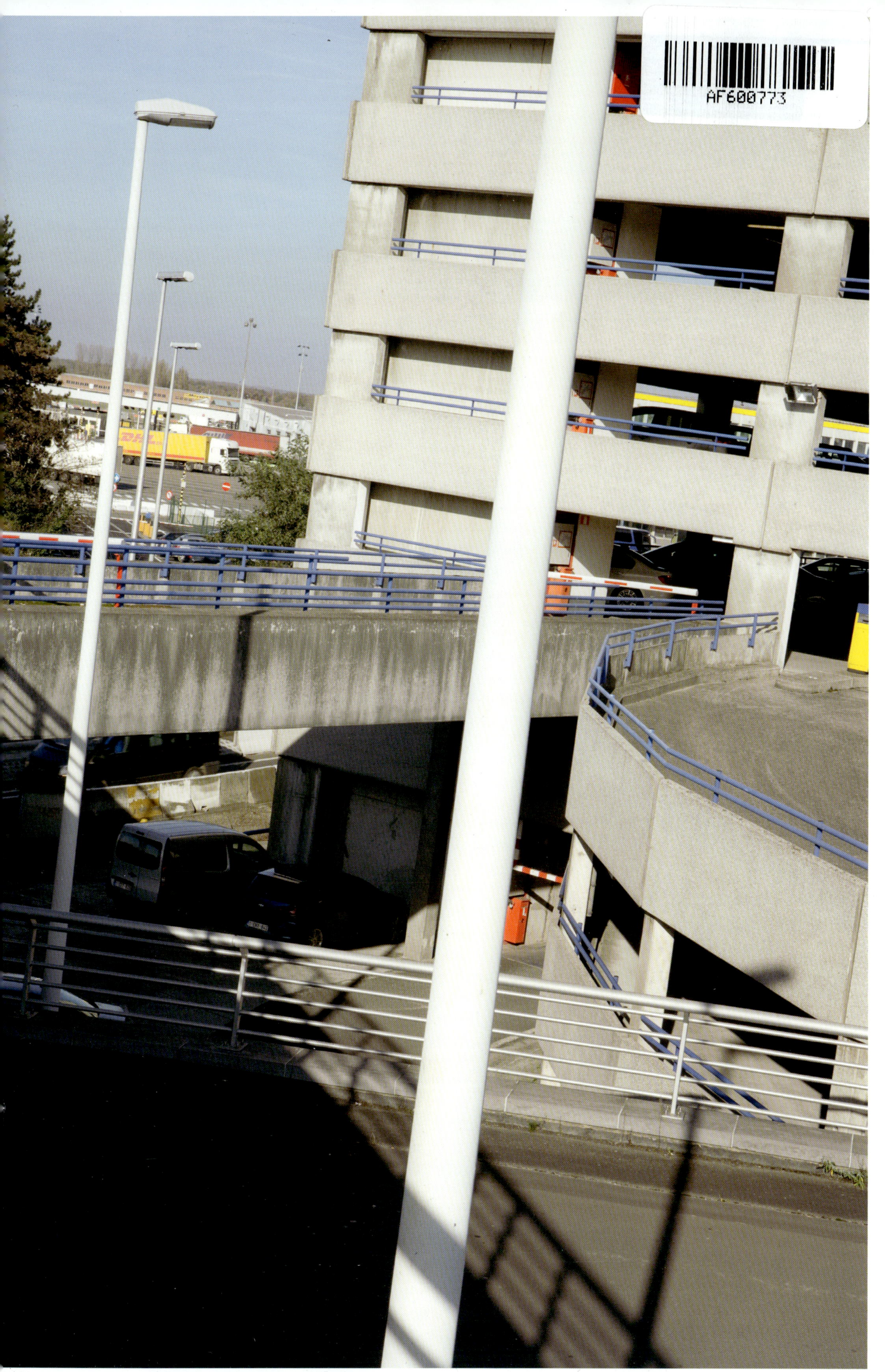

AF600773

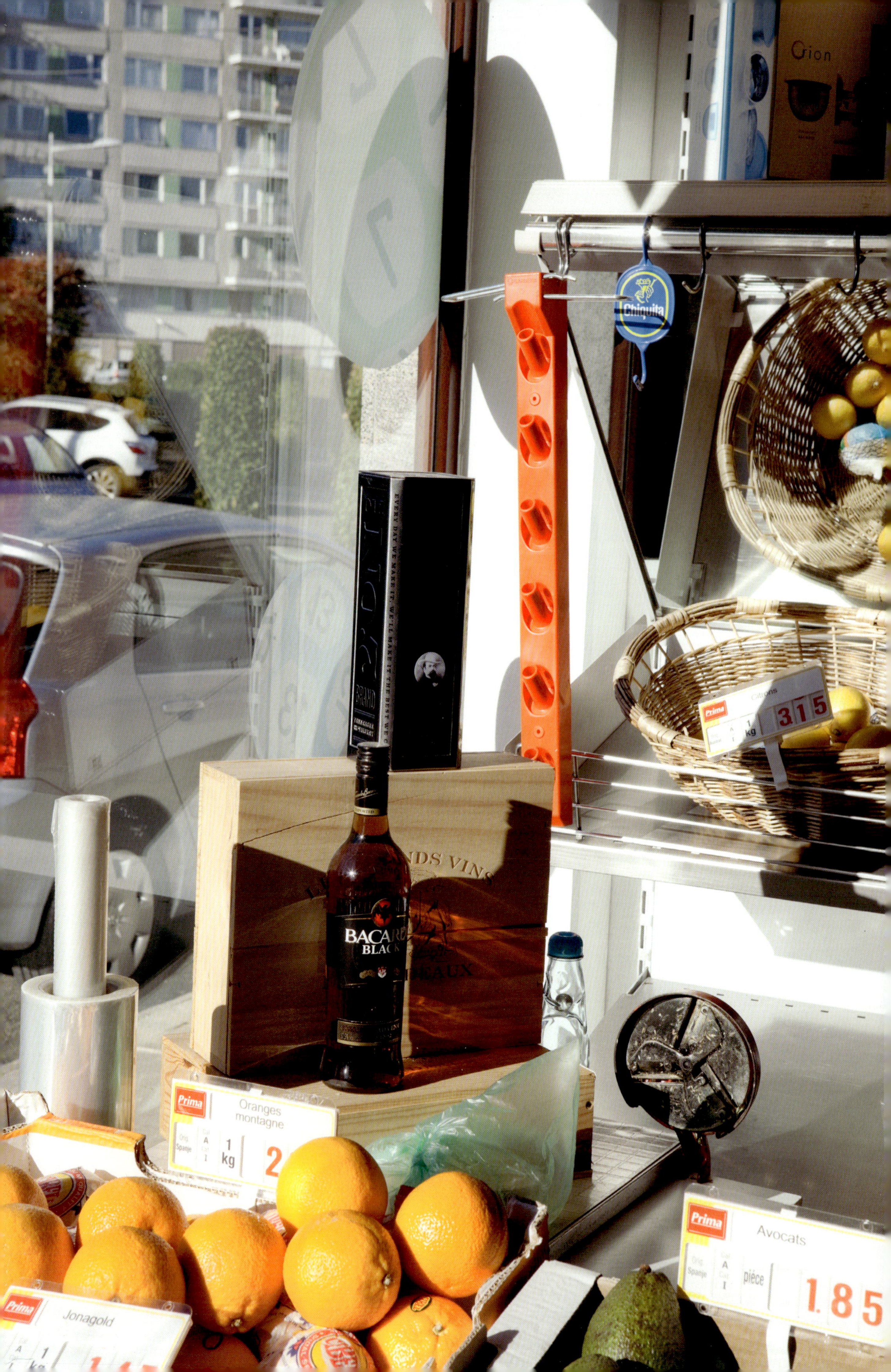
Chiquita
Prima
315
BACARDI
BLACK
Prima
Oranges
montagne
1
kg
2
Prima
Avocats
pièce
1.85
Prima
Jonagold

The outskirts of Brussels. An extremely complex area where residential, recreational and commercial functions clash harshly with one another. A densely-branched network of motorways, a series of interminable, straight main roads and an airport give access to the region and structure the landscape: they are the axes around which these functions are arranged. And there, right through the middle of it all, an imposing old forest that stretches out across a large part of the area.

In her exploration of this area, Stephanie Kiwitt opts not for a connecting horizontal view, but for a vertical cross-section. Not for the broad juxtaposition that offers an explanation, but for the narrow, isolating incision. The detached approach that aims mainly for an overview is here replaced by a direct, almost physical contact. She does not concentrate on the question of spatial cluttering, but records how her body reacts to these indefinable places. The rigid frame of the erect image refers to the verticality of the pedestrian, while the broad overview of the horizontal image corresponds to what the driver sees through his windscreen. The one experiences the landscape as an accumulation of incongruous (but also intriguing) fragments, while the other comprehends it pragmatically as a space through which one just has to pass. The one looks at his surroundings with curiosity, while the other navigates through it with a purpose (and above all as fast as possible).

The outskirts of the city are an in-between zone through which one passes on the way into or out of the city. But these photos are at odds with this dynamic. They do not keep to the vanishing point of the straight main roads, but stubbornly turn away from the traffic, focus on blank walls, on fences, on obstacles, on the pavement, on a roller shutter. They turn obstinately towards what only the pedestrian can notice. And just as the pedestrian's attention is focused on what immediately surrounds him, these pictures come strikingly close to their subjects. With no appreciable depth, but with plenty of concrete and brick, little sky and almost always lacking a liberating horizon, they advance an obtrusive proximity.

A rigid frame, an insistent directness, barely any room to move, and yet they are not claustrophobic pictures. The viewer never feels jammed into a hermetically sealed space. This is the consequence of two strategies. Firstly a deliberate intervention in the formal construction of the image. A clever interplay of repetition and variation makes sure that the elements of the image are positioned in an exciting relationship with each other. Secondly: use of a highly mobile camera, swishing from side to side and sometimes even leaning over frightfully to the left or right. This unstable, oblique view suggests a fleeting touch rather than any desire to pin down what has been seen. Both strategies confirm the refusal to make any imperative statements *about* this landscape. These are not topographic positions, but playful and adventurous rearrangements of planes, lines and colours to form a new and previously unseen landscape.

Steven Humblet

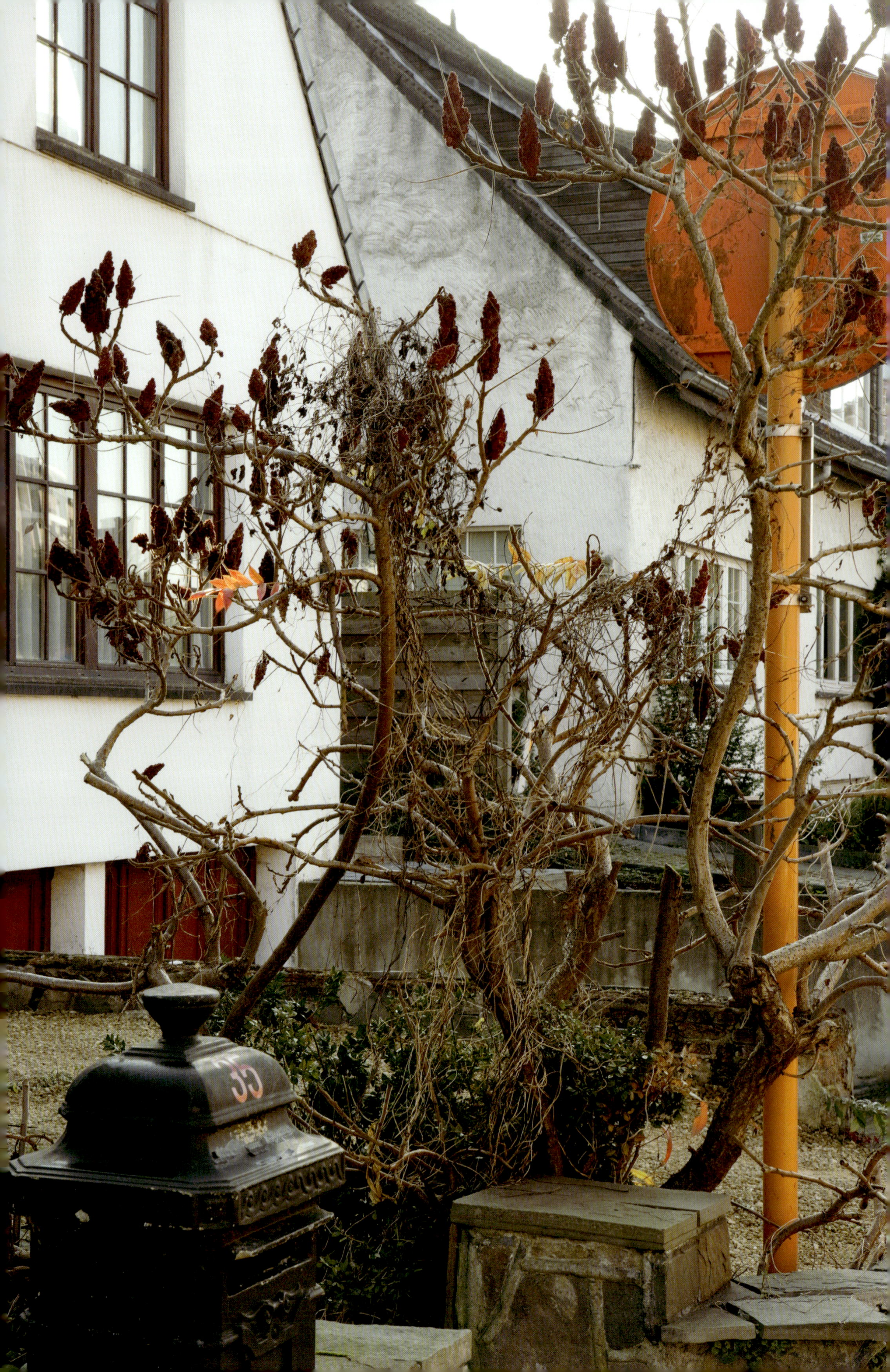
35

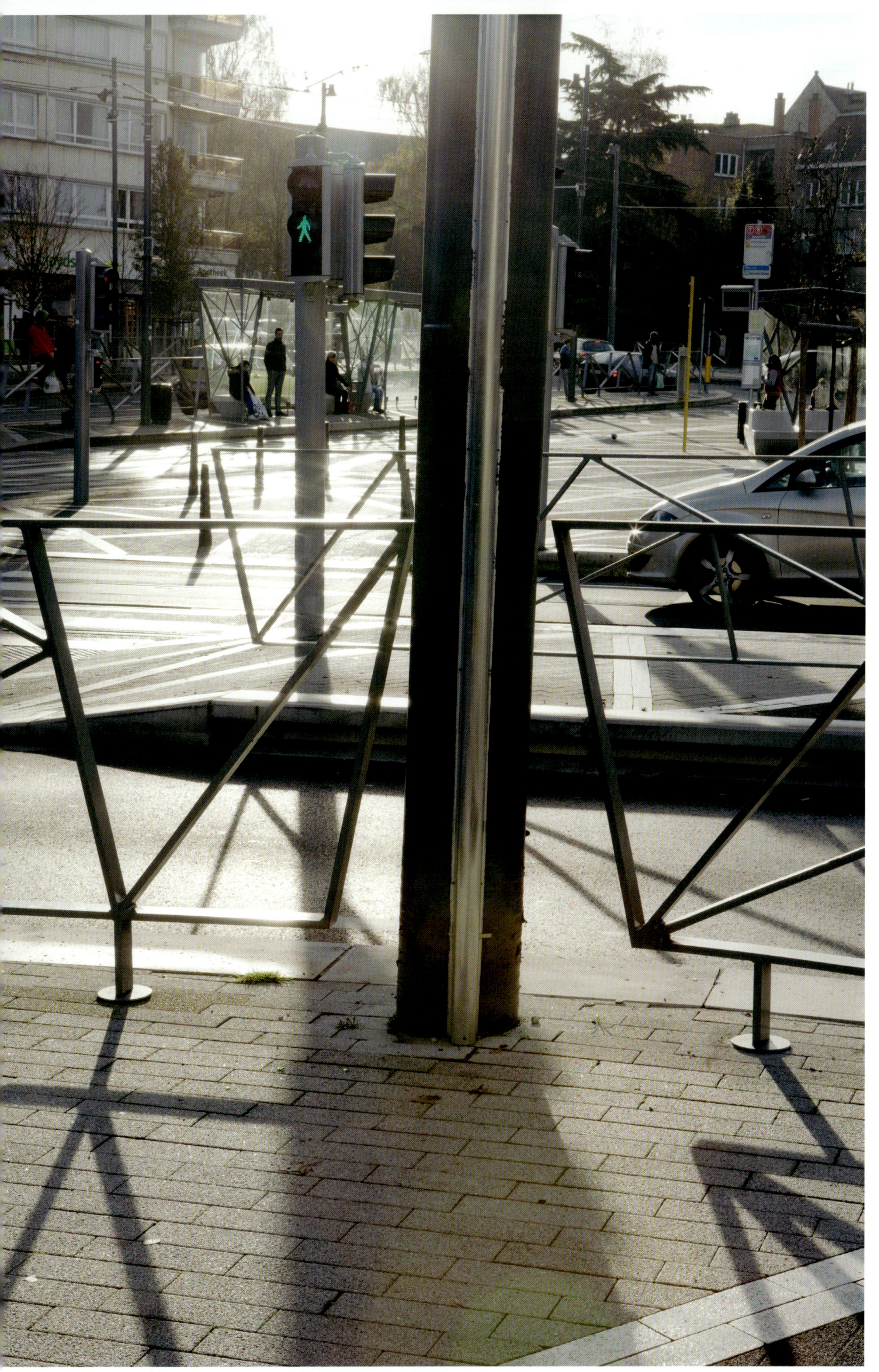

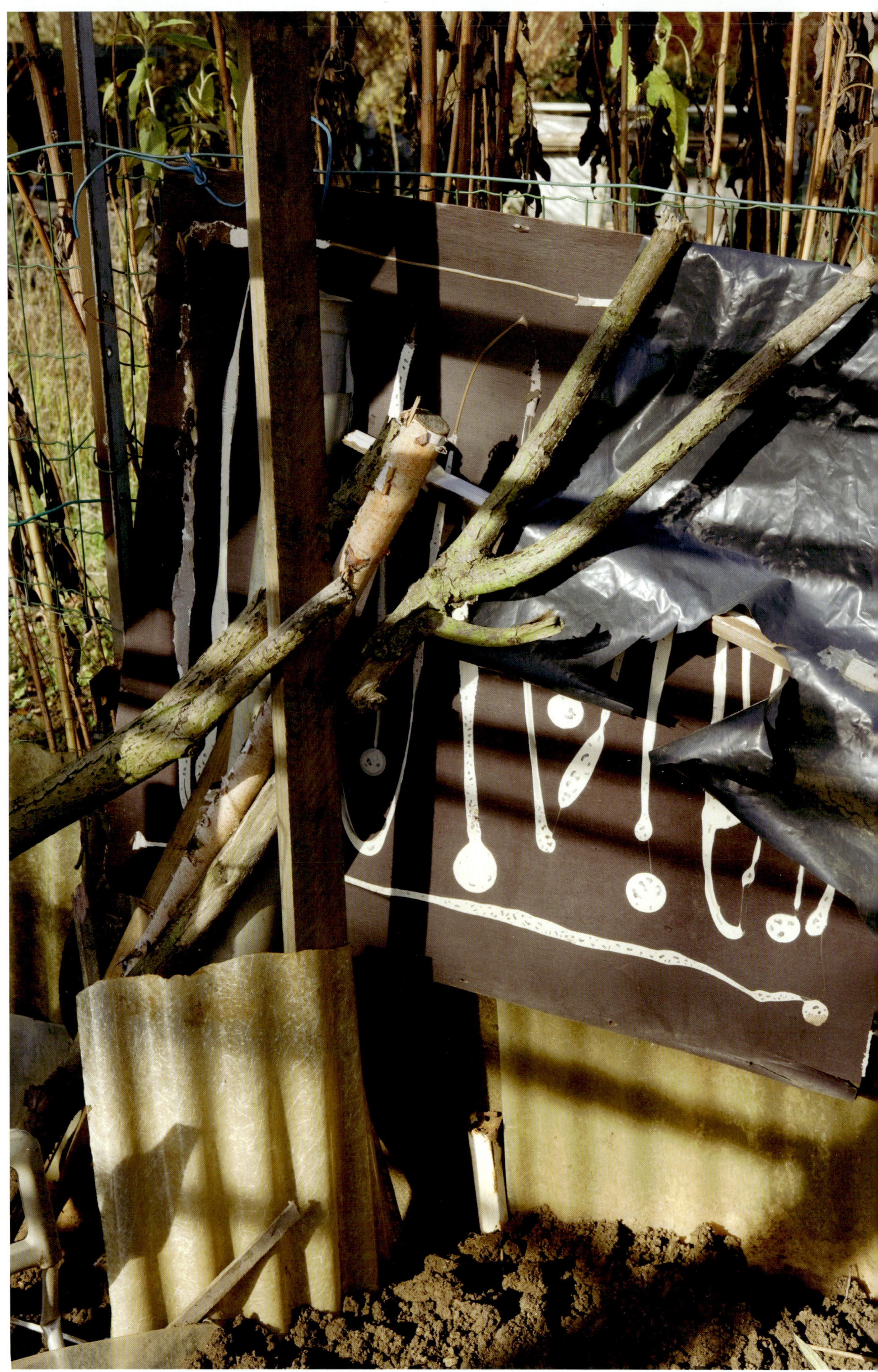

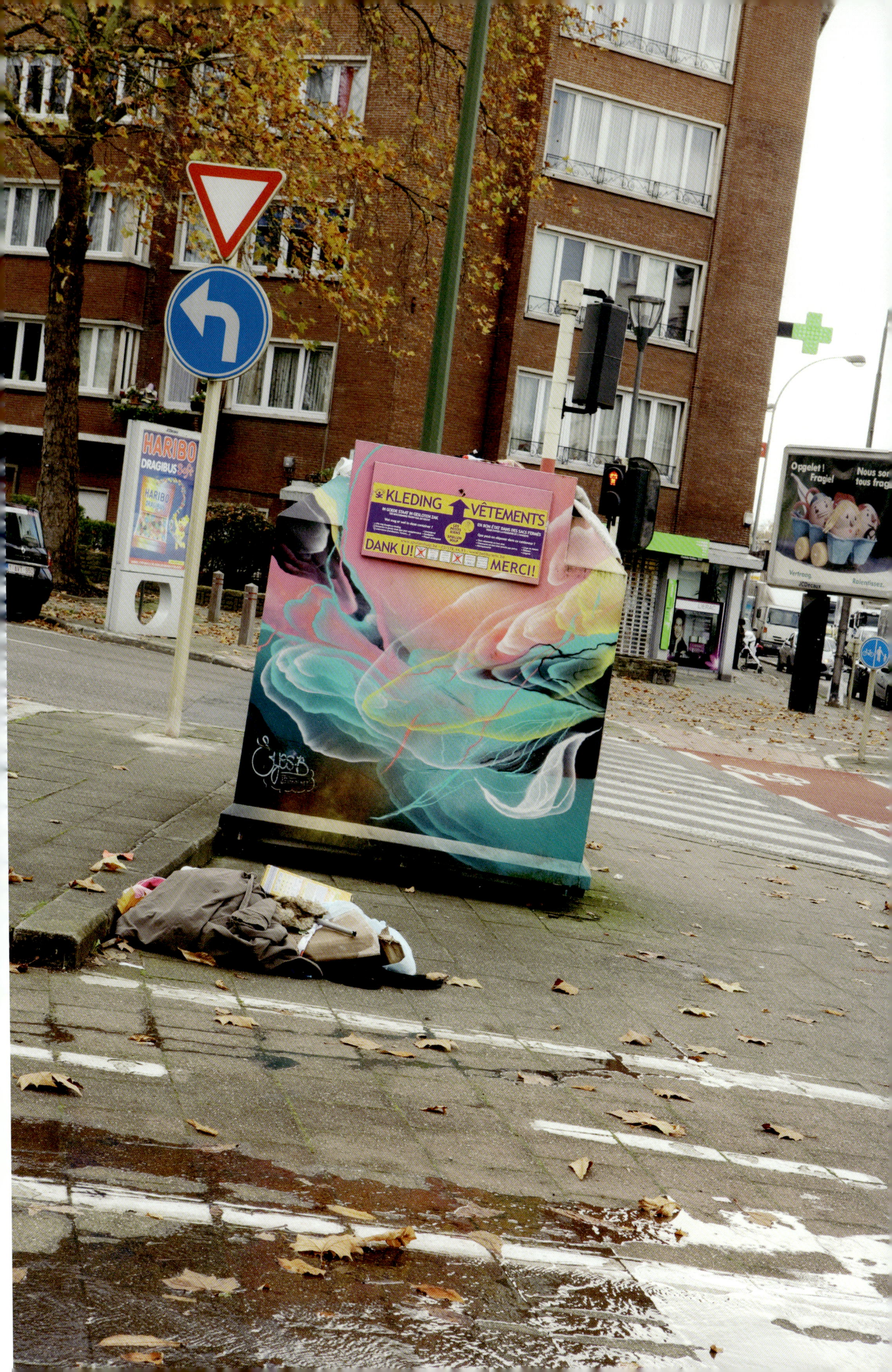
HARIBO
DRAGIBUS
KLEDING
VÊTEMENTS
IN GOEDE STAAT IN GESLOTEN ZAK
EN BON ÉTAT DANS DES SACS FERMÉS
LES PETITS BIENS
SPULLENHULP
DANK U!
MERCI!
Opgelet!
Fragiel
Vertraag.
JCDecaux
Ralentissez.

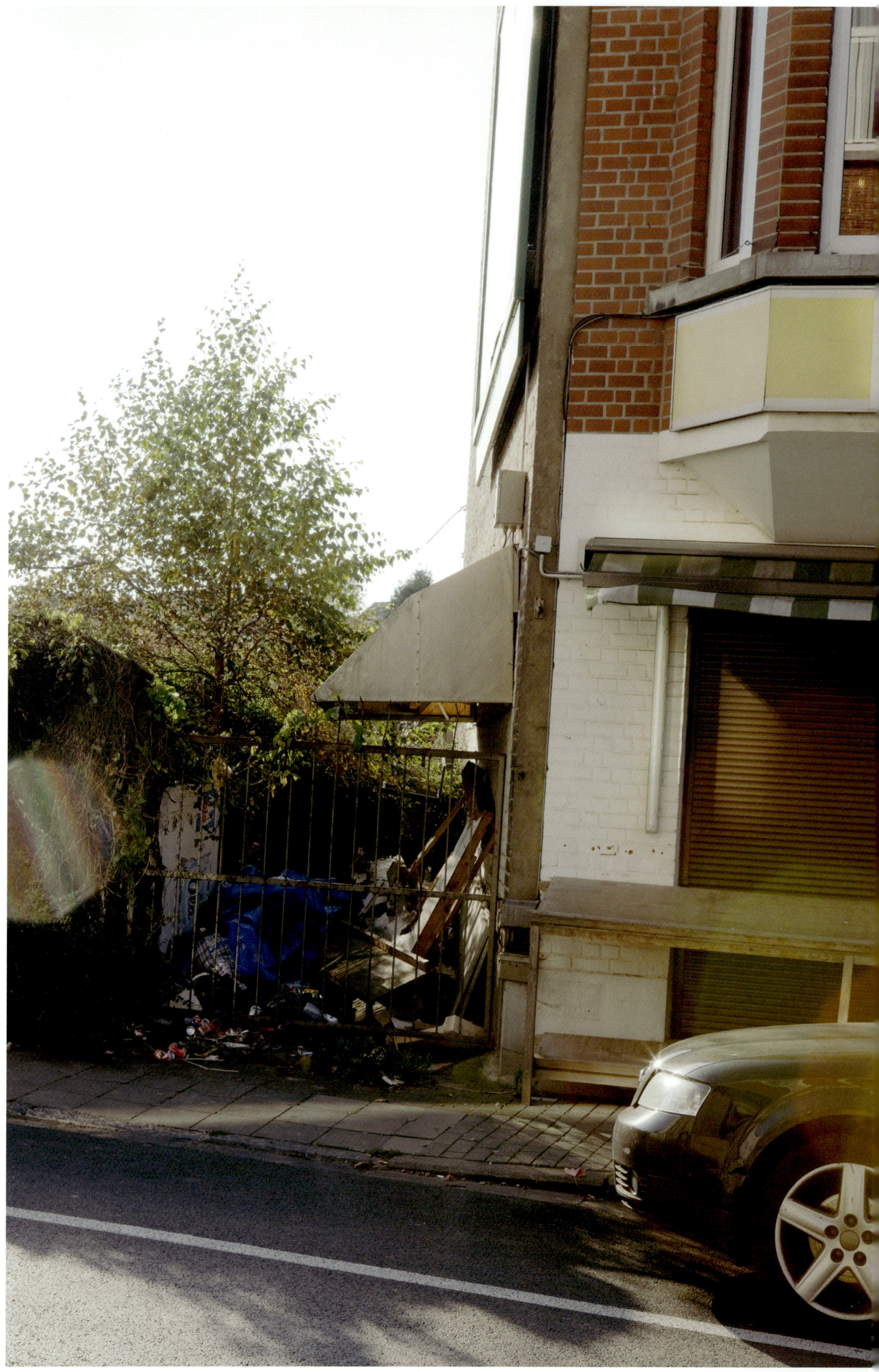

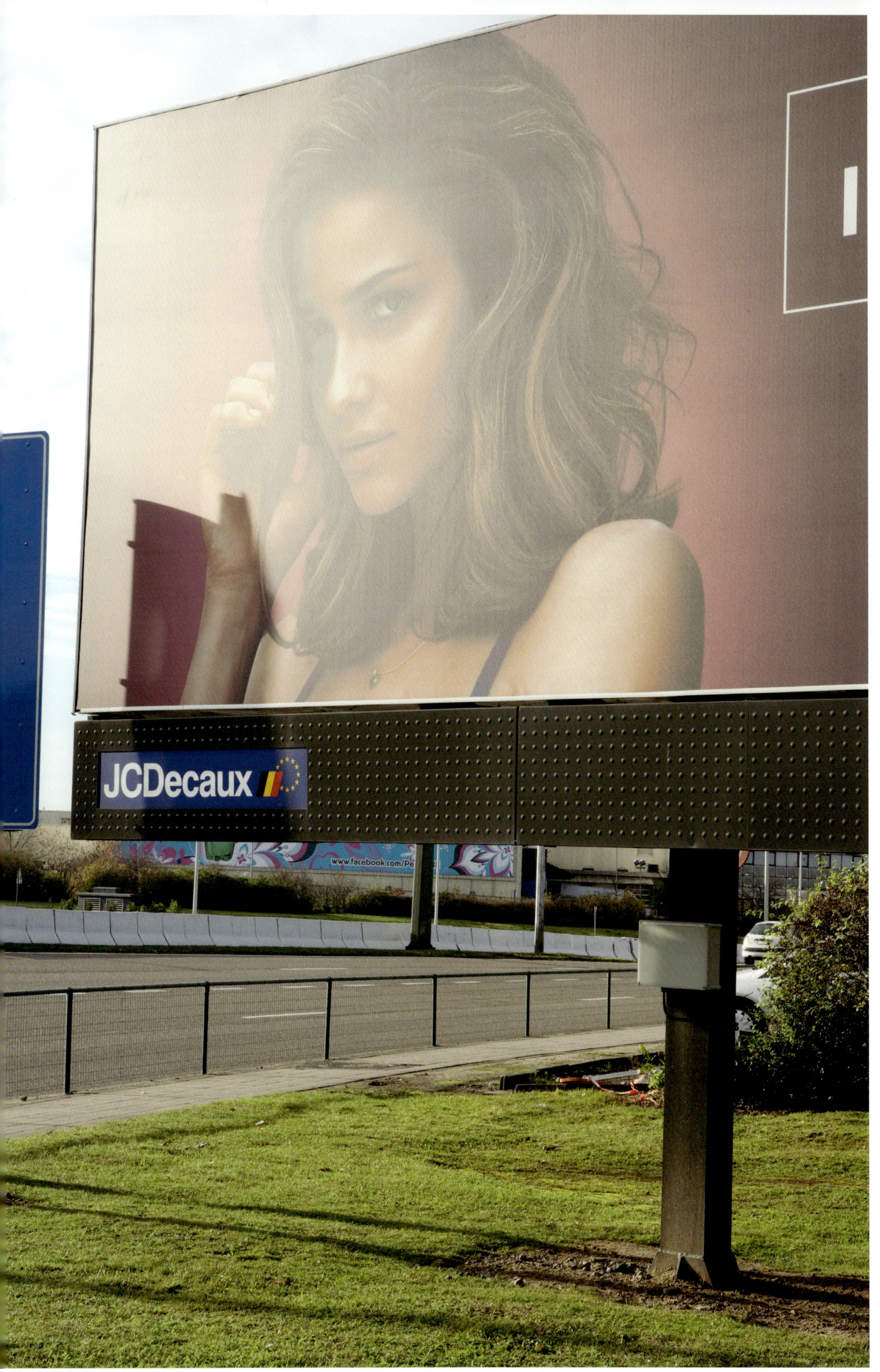
JCDecaux

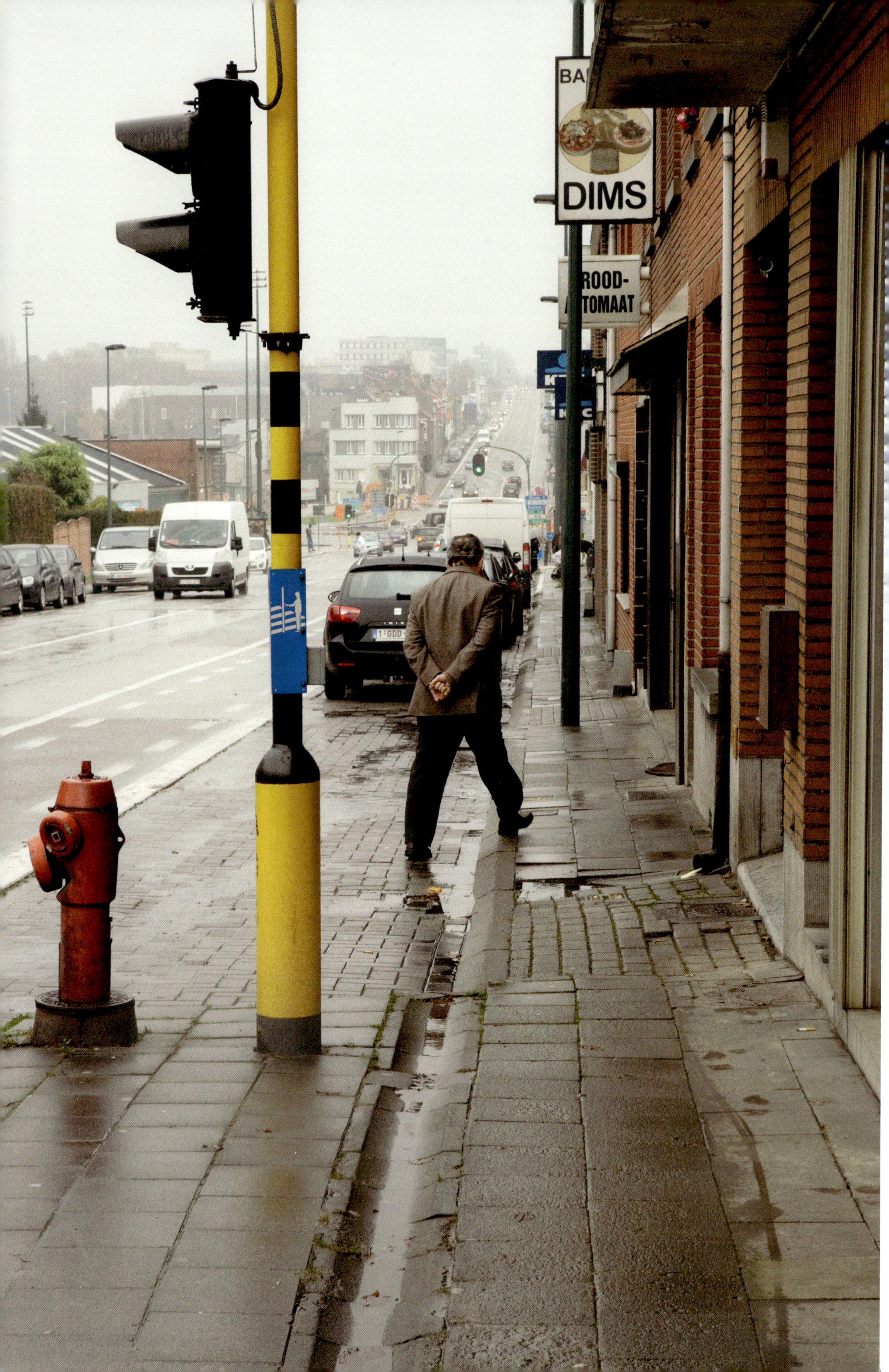
BA
DIMS
ROOD-
TOMAAT

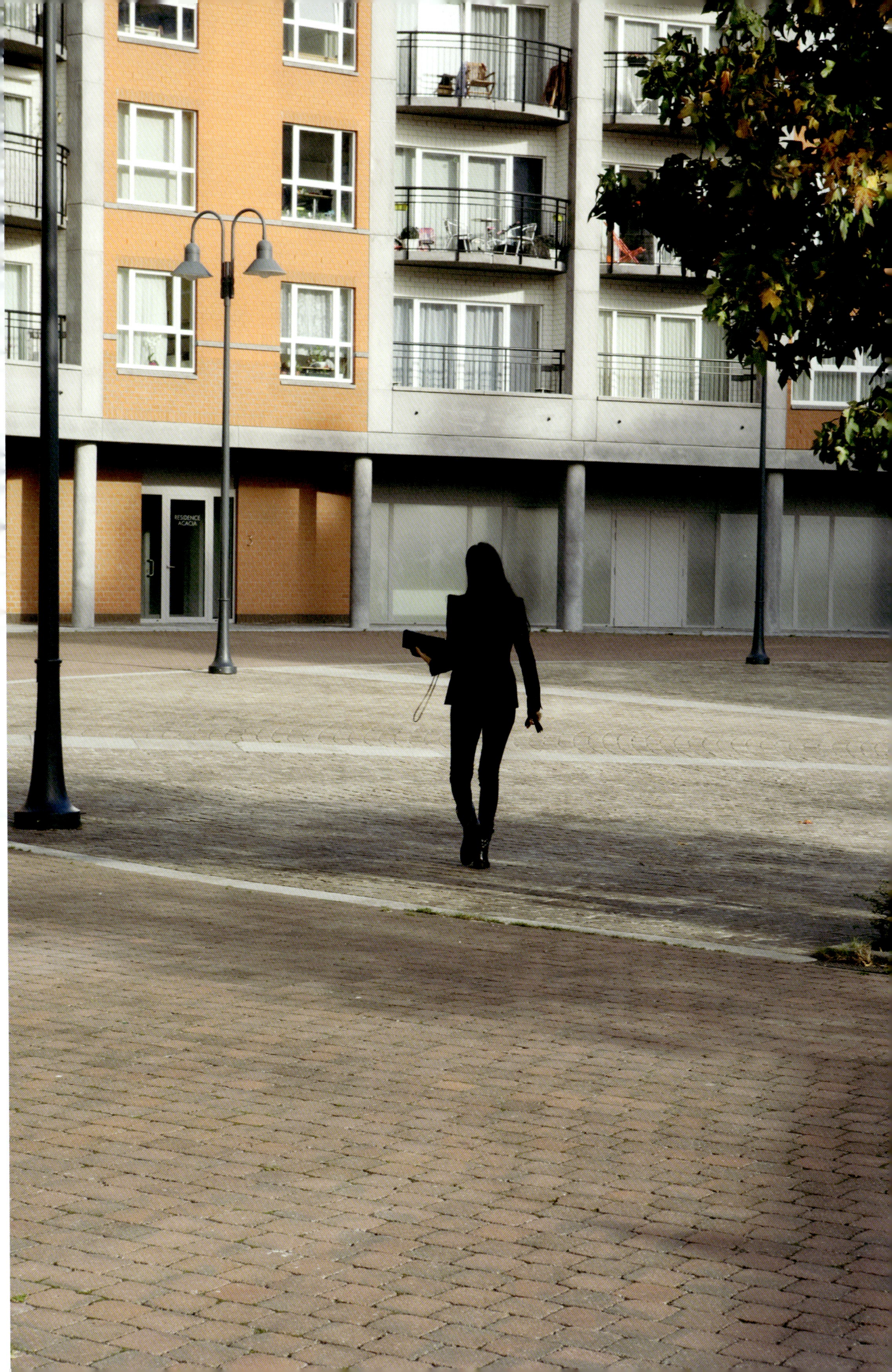
RESIDENCE
ACACIA

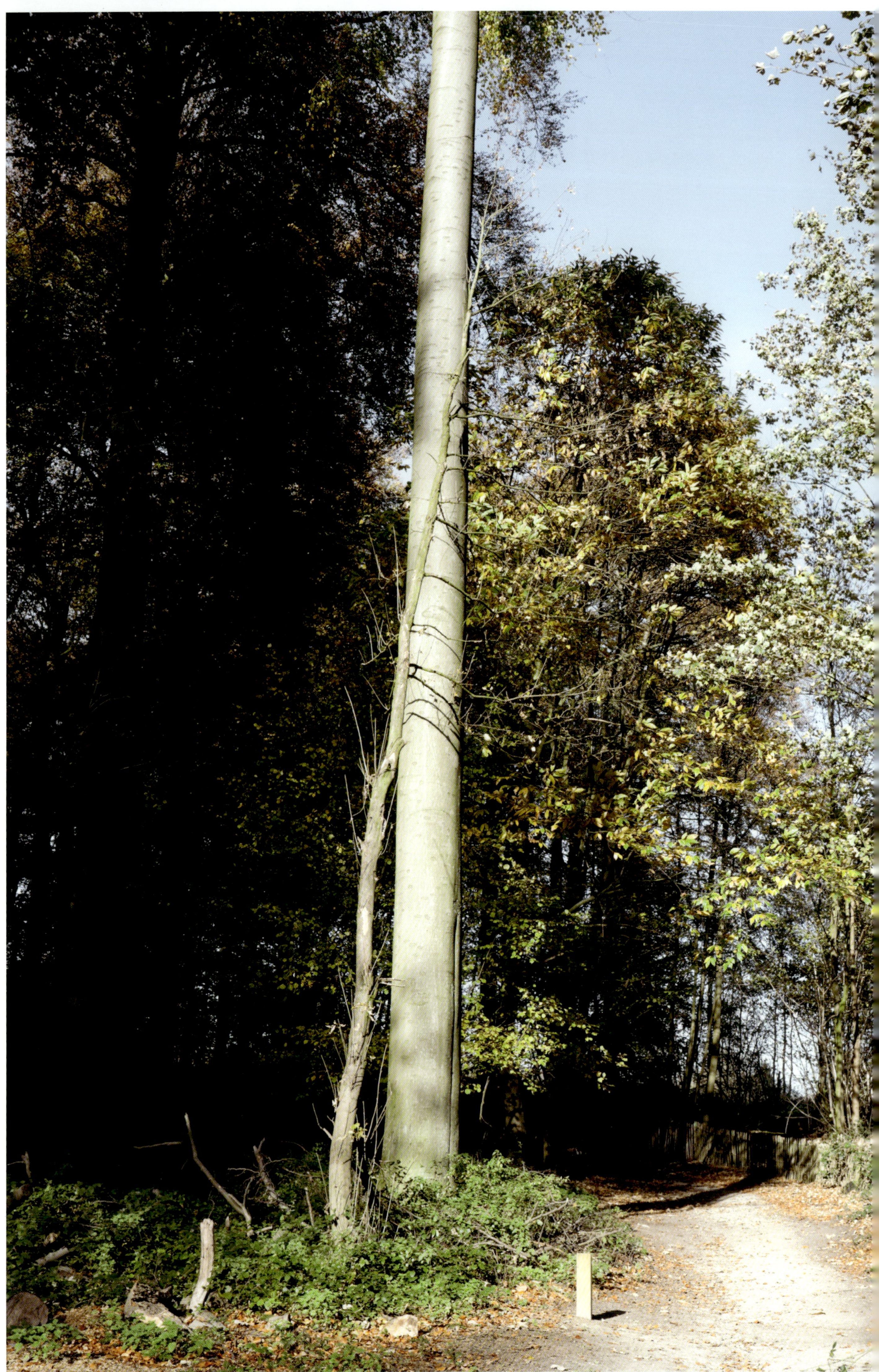

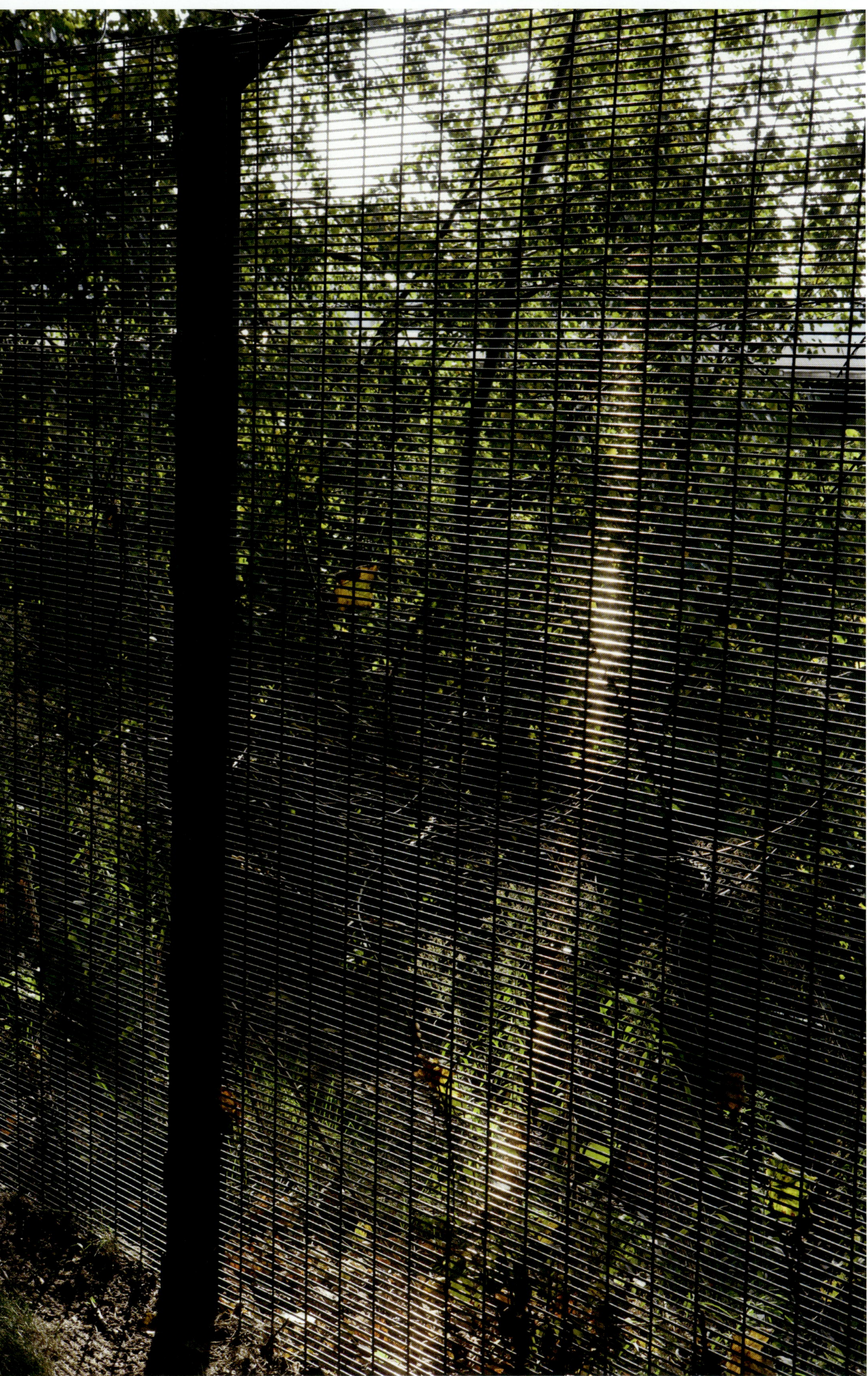

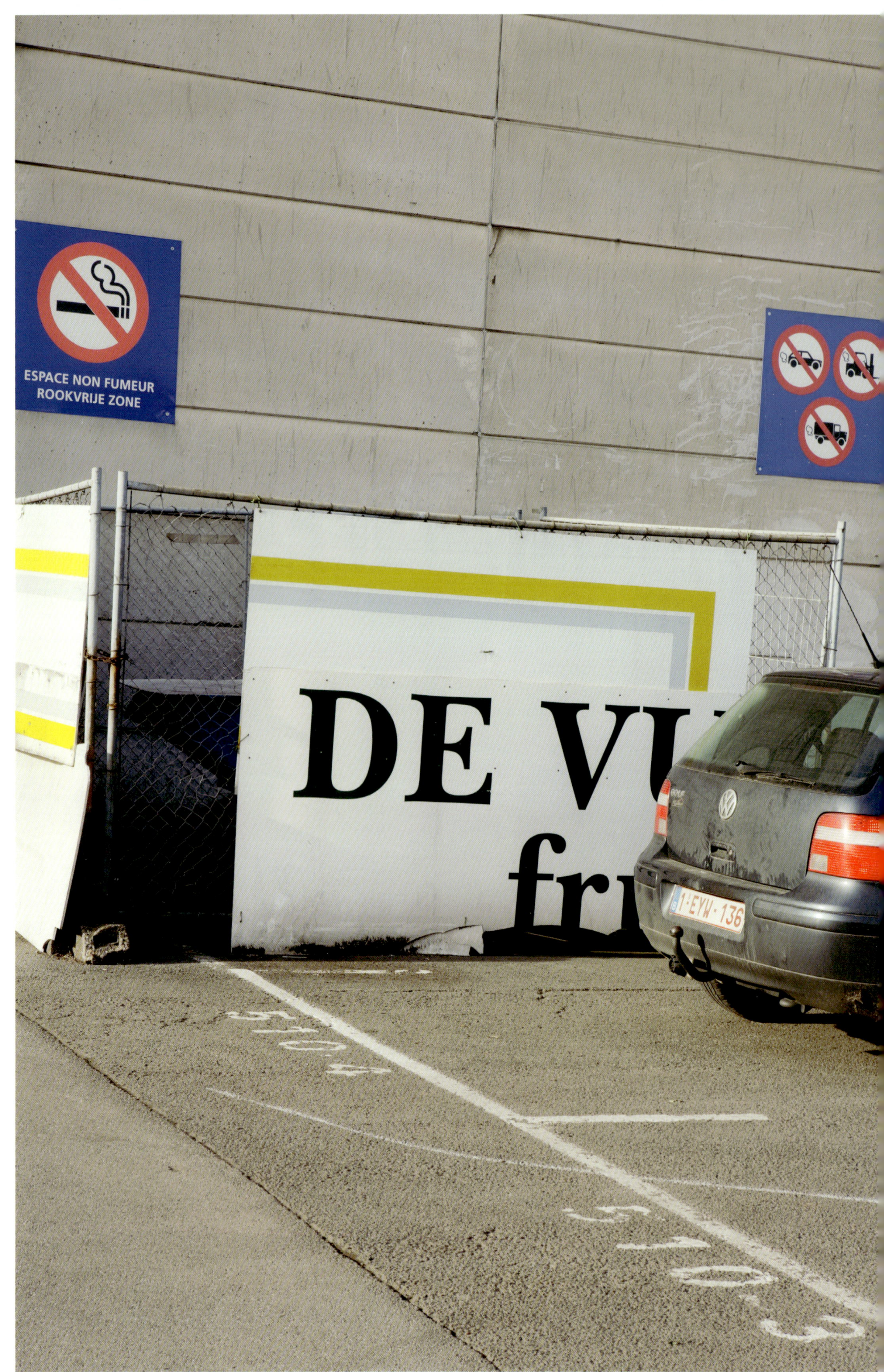
ESPACE NON FUMEUR
ROOKVRIJE ZONE
DE V

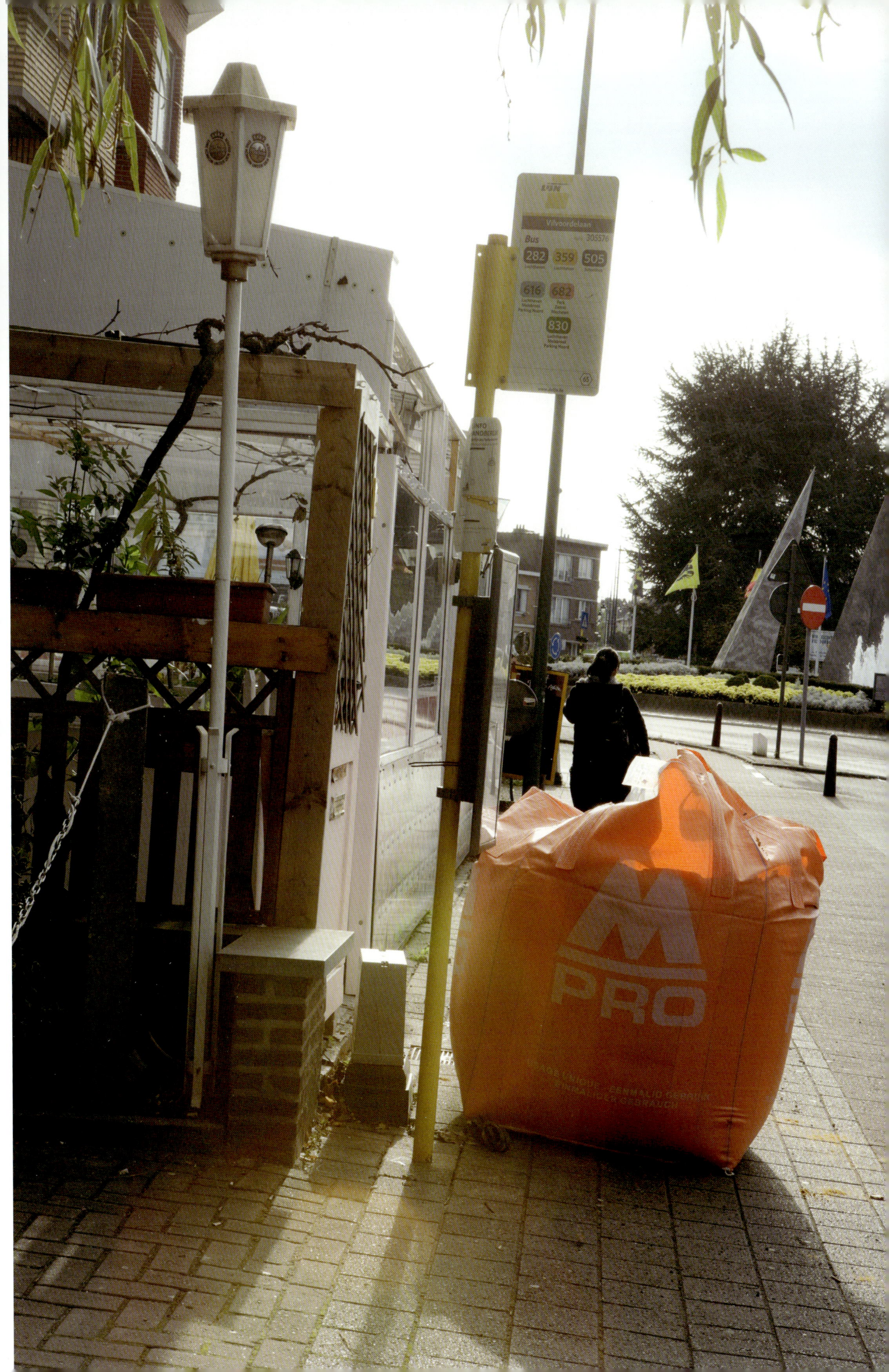
Vilvoordelaan
Bus
282
359
505
616
682
830
M
PRO

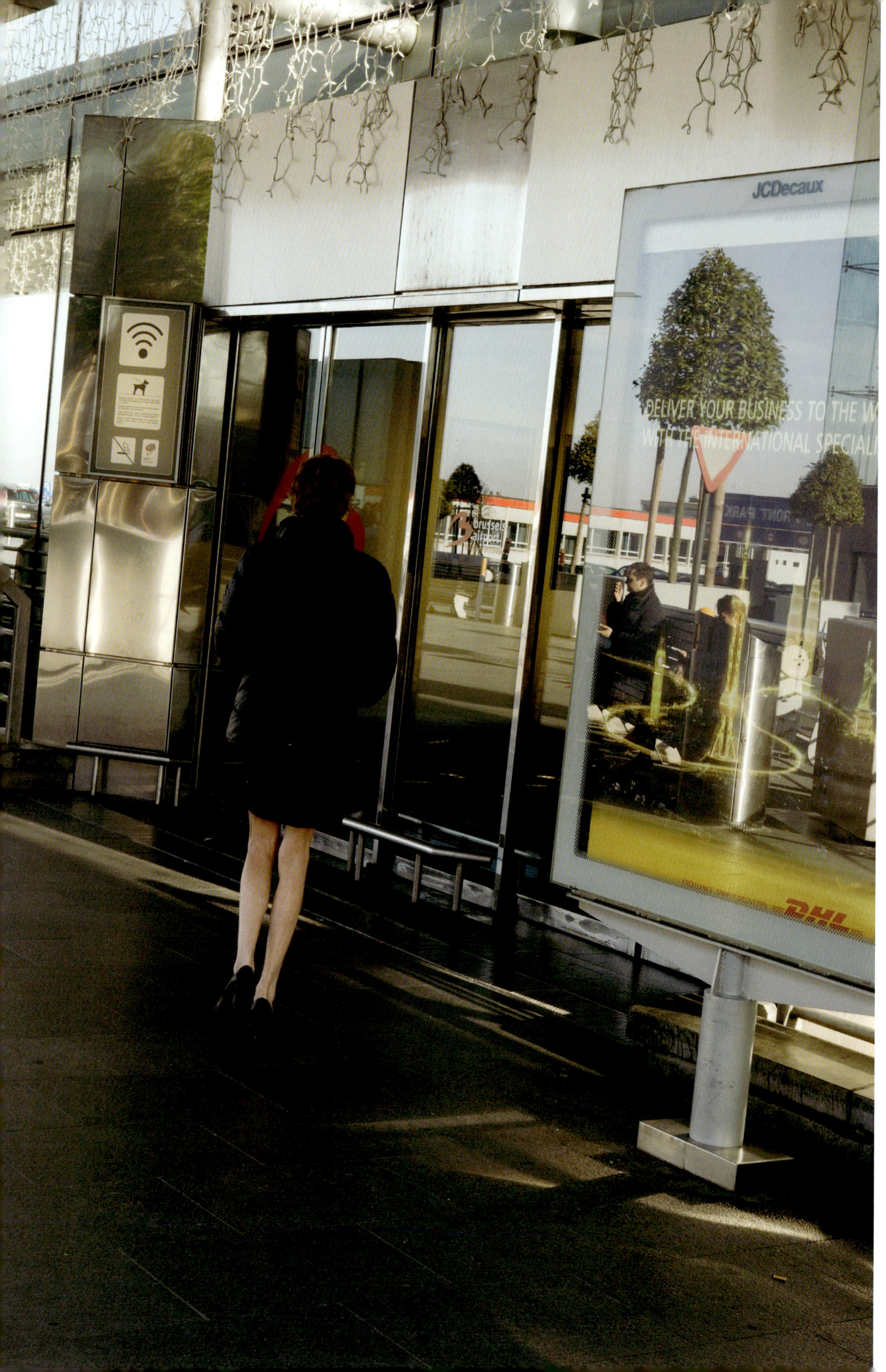
JCDecaux
DELIVER YOUR BUSINESS TO THE
WITH THE INTERNATIONAL
brussels airport
DHL

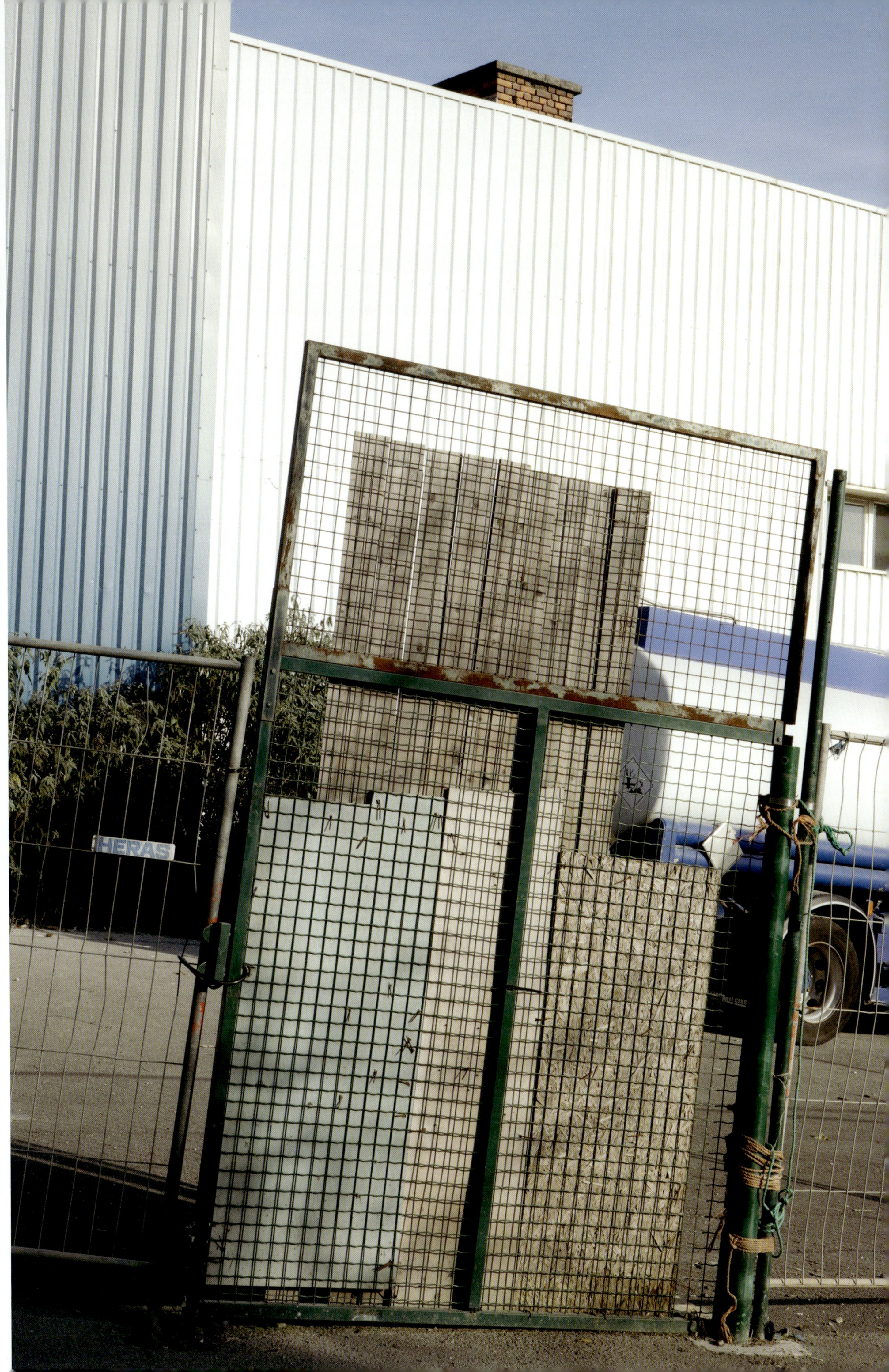
HERAS

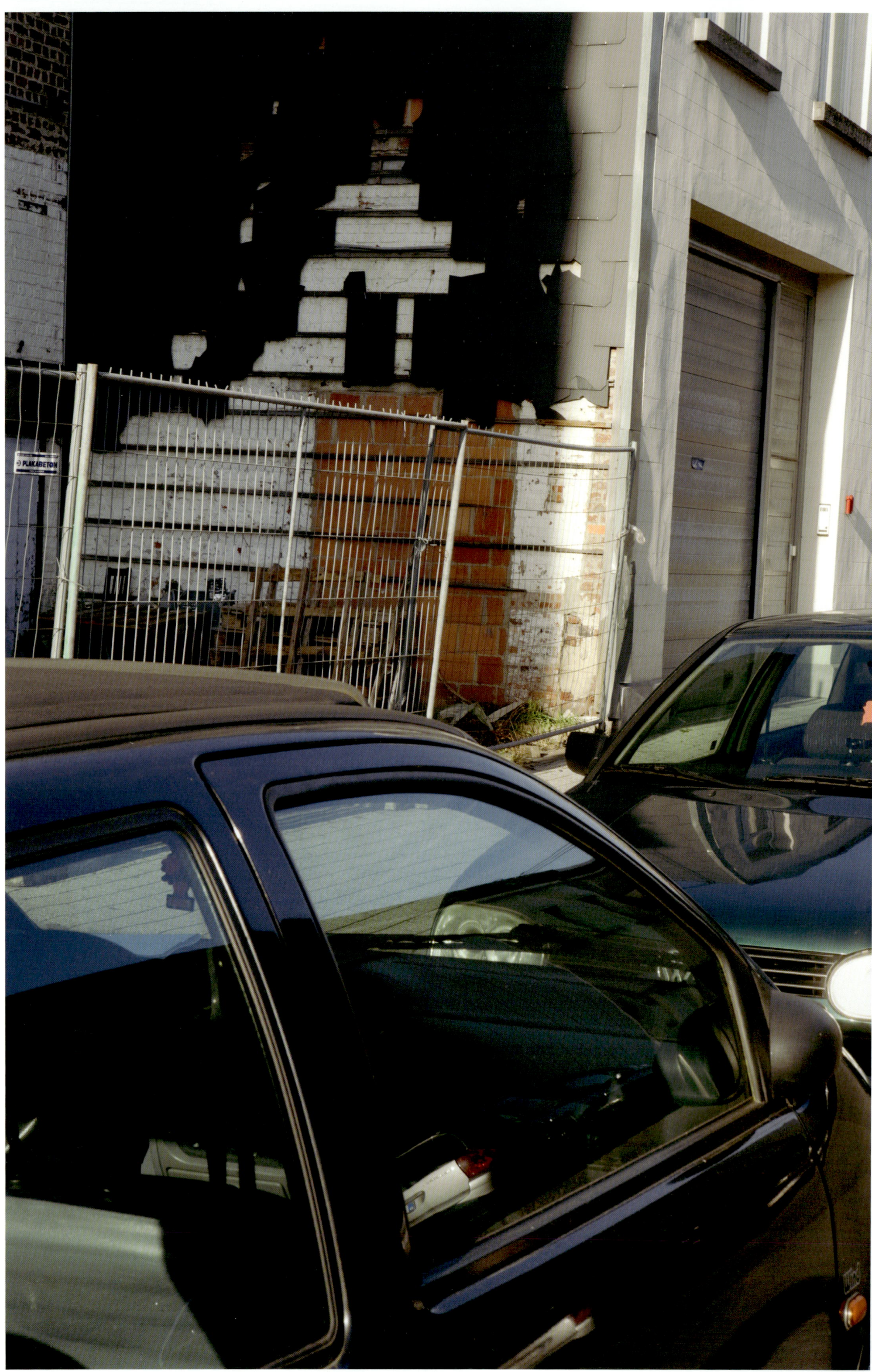
PLAKABETON

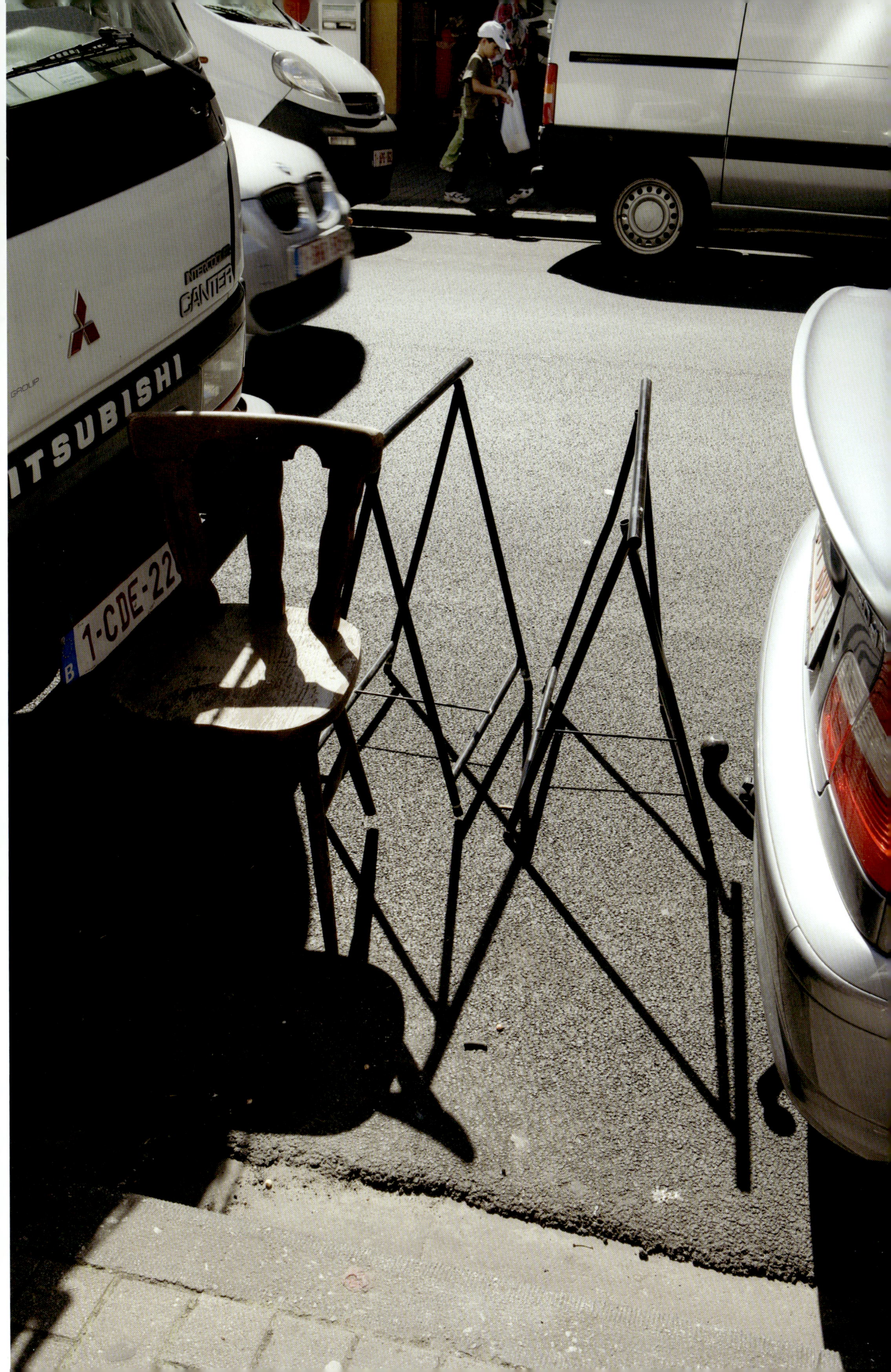

CANTER
ITSUBISHI
GROUP
1-CDE-22
B

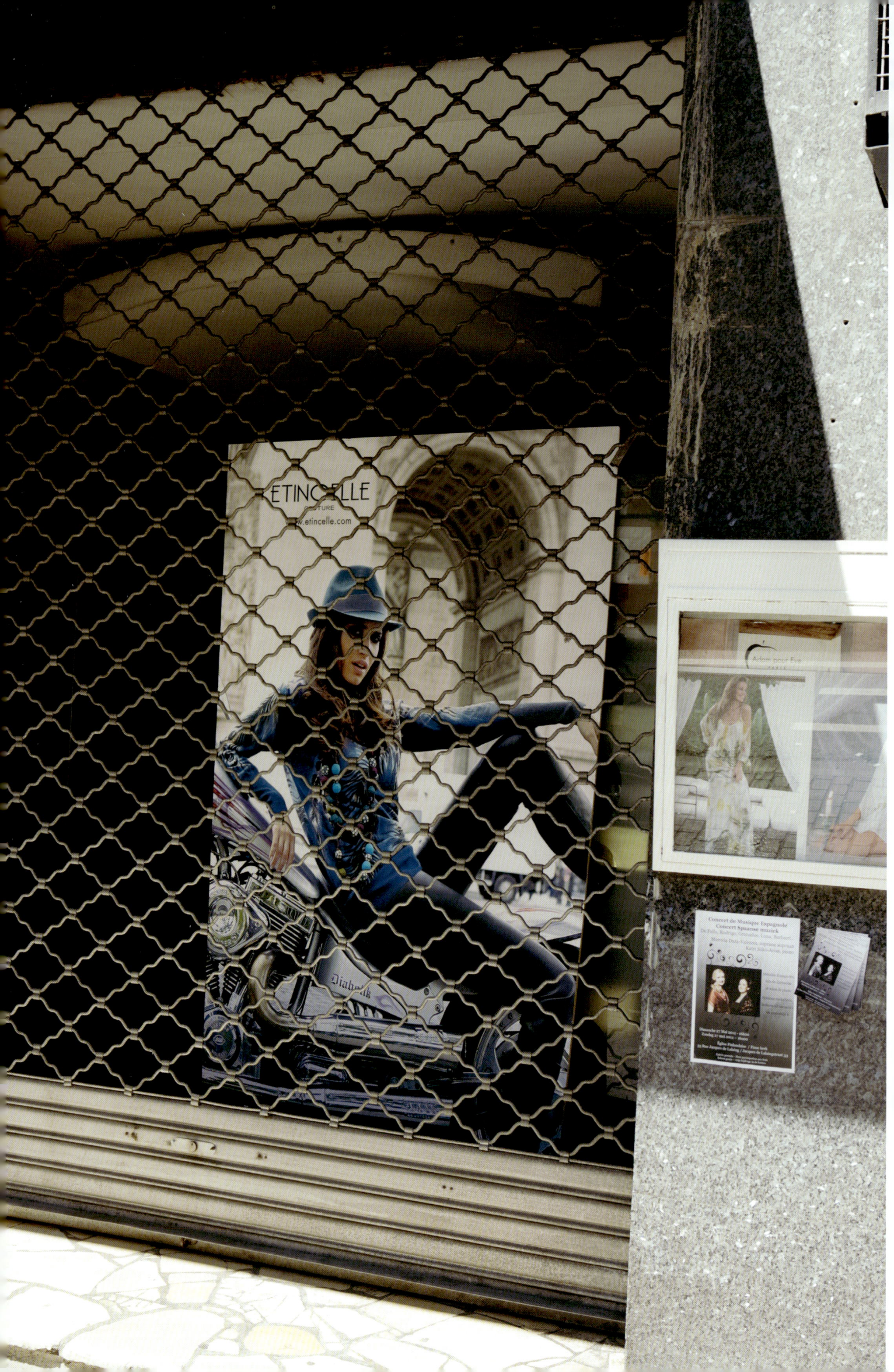
ETINCELLE
w.etincelle.com
Concert de Musique Espagnole
Concert Spaanse muziek

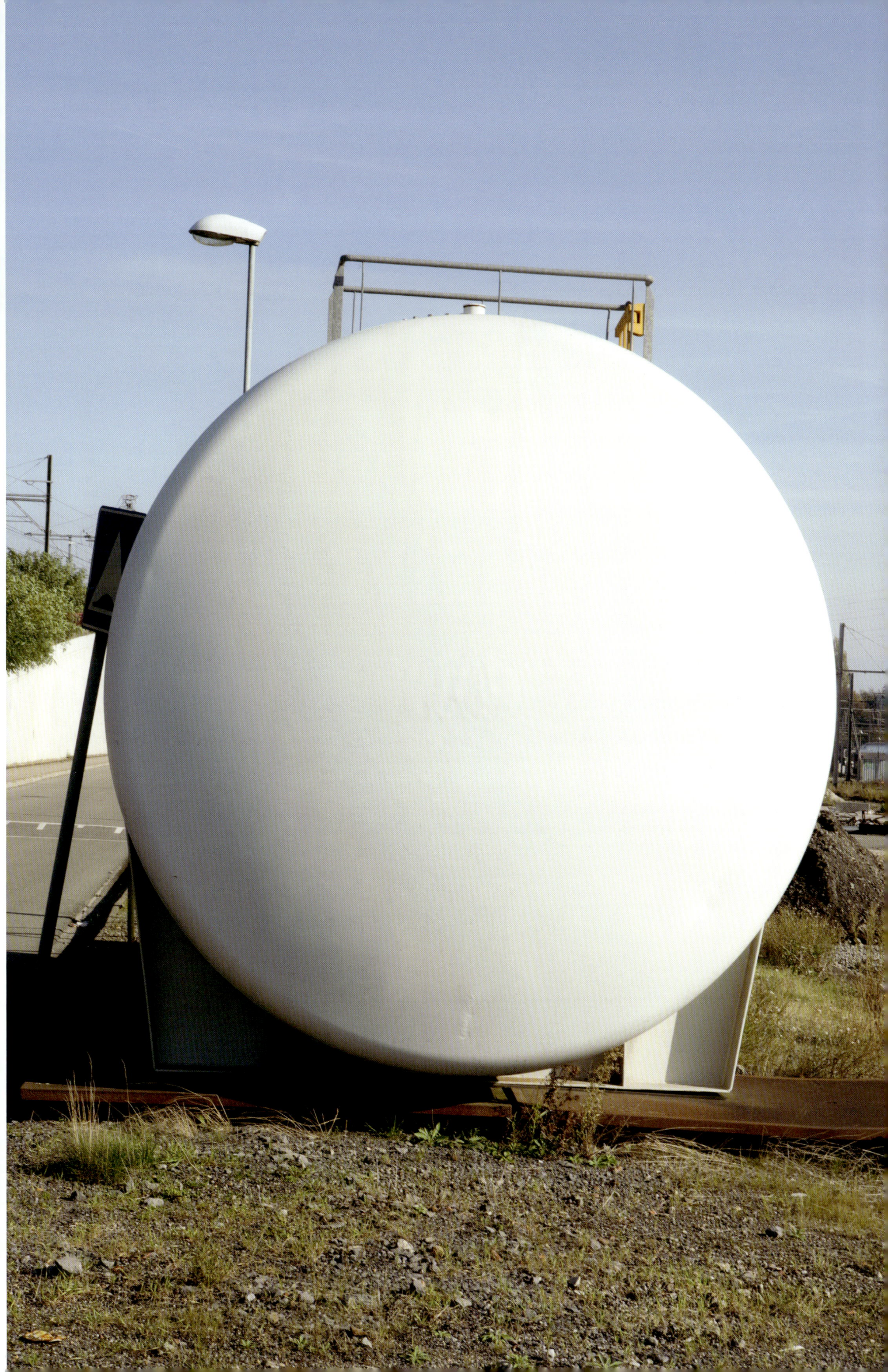

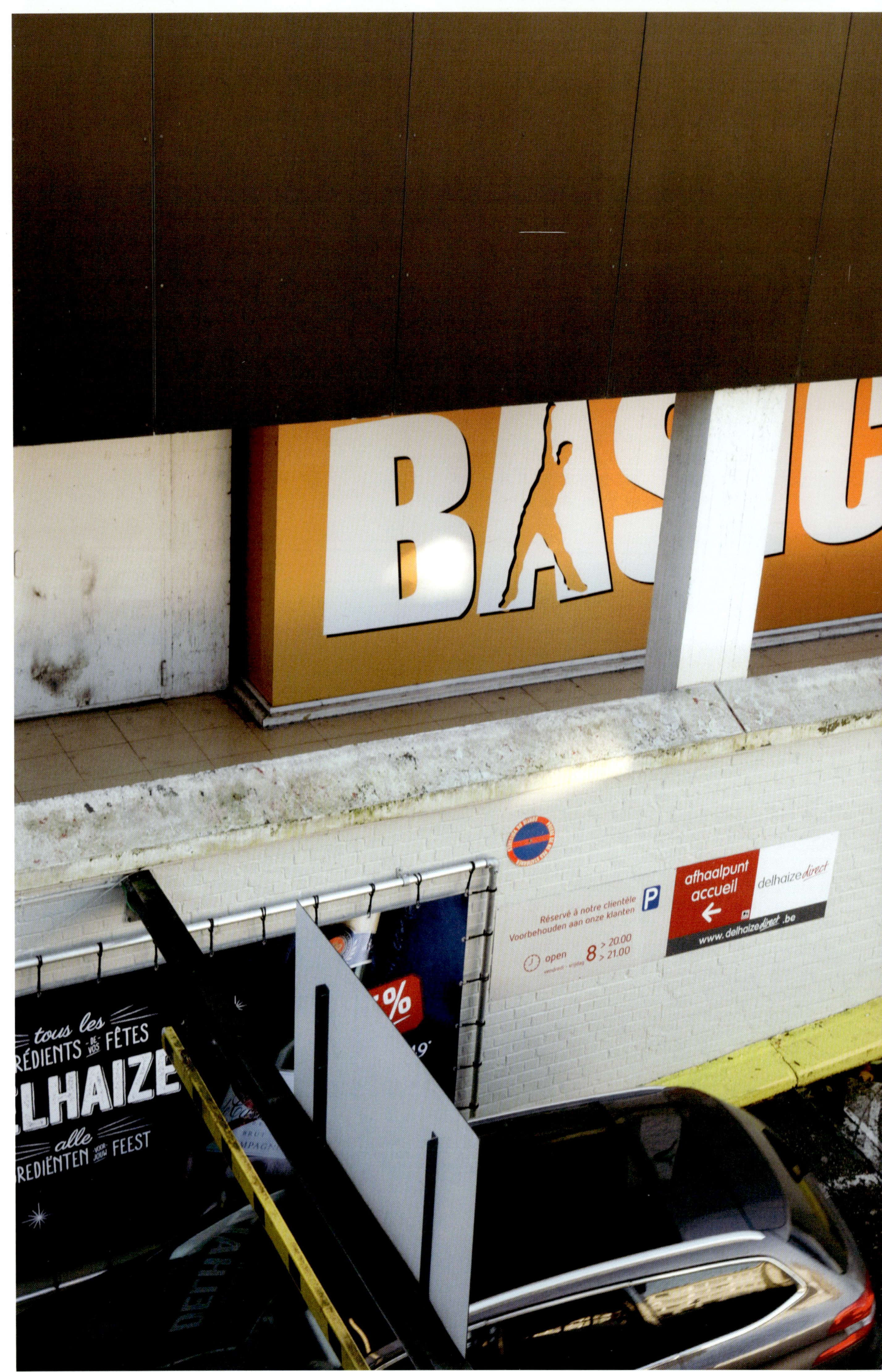
BASIC
Réservé à notre clientèle
Voorbehouden aan onze klanten
P
open
8 > 20.00
> 21.00
afhaalpunt
accueil
delhaize direct
www.delhaize direct .be
tous les
RÉDIENTS DE VOS FÊTES
LHAIZE
alle
REDIËNTEN VOOR JOUW FEEST

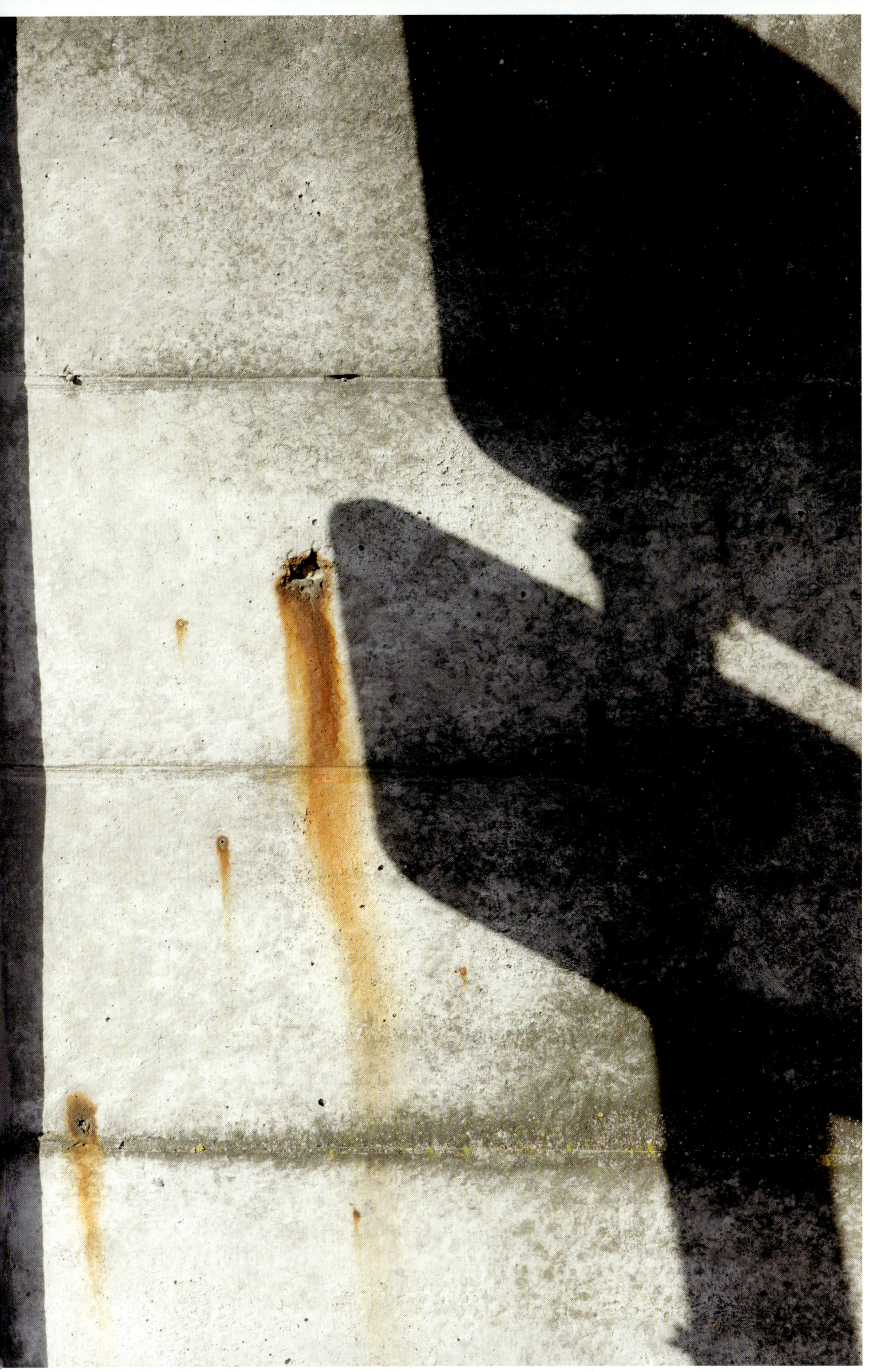

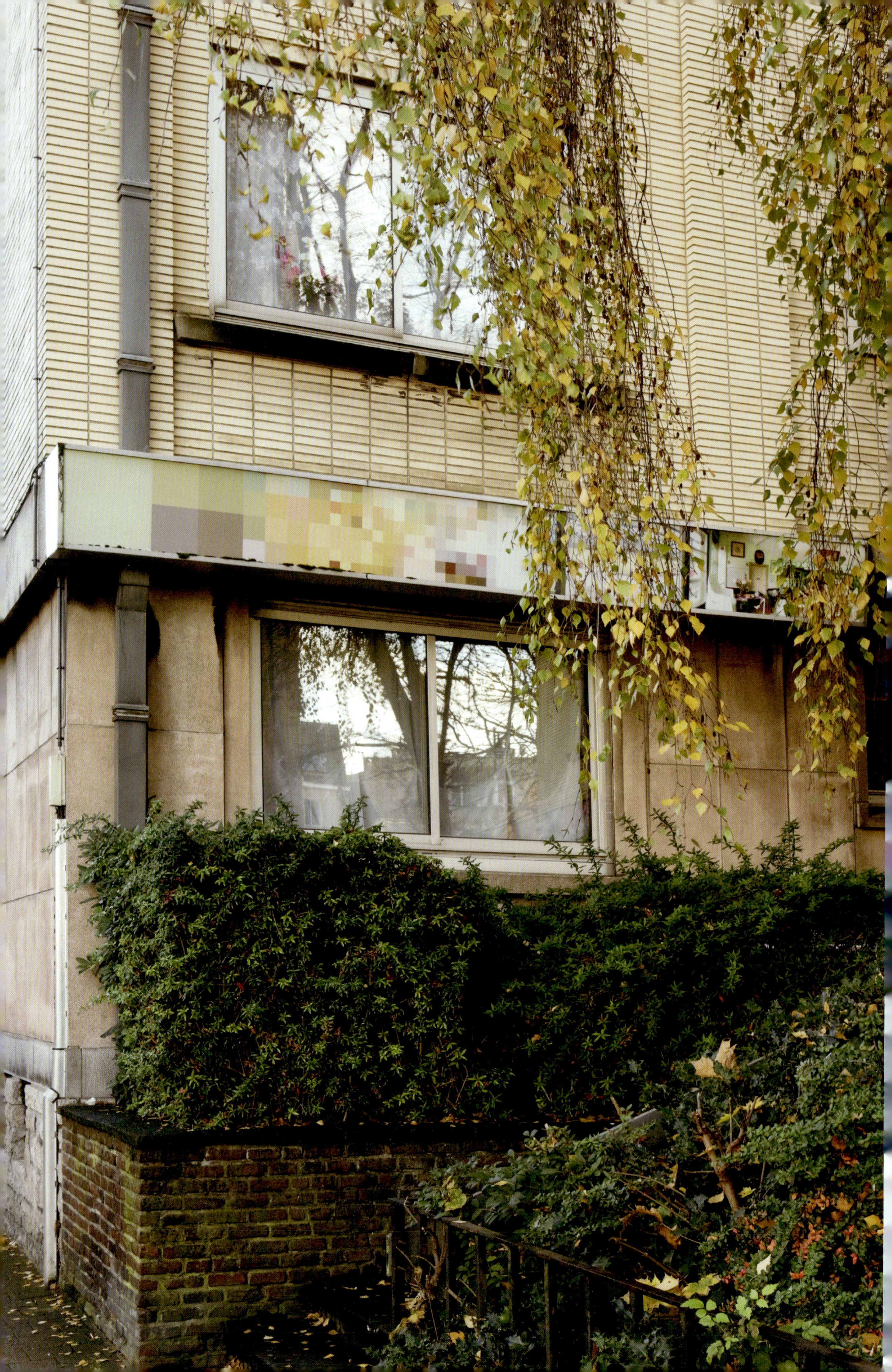

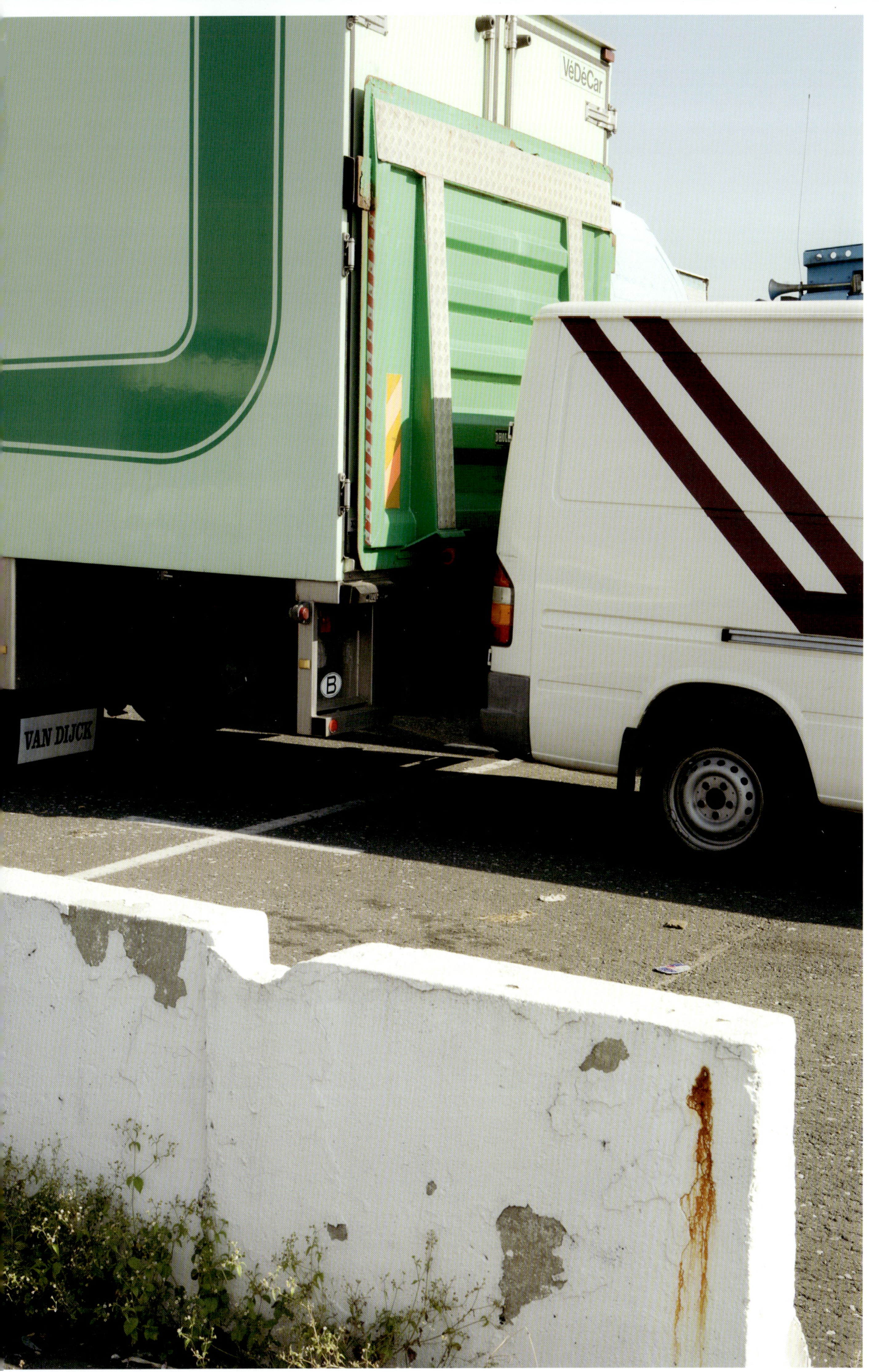
VéDéCar
VAN DIJCK
B

APE#056
Stephanie Kiwitt, Four Oranges,
Some Office Buildings, Woman's Legs
© 2015, Art Paper Editions
& Stephanie Kiwitt
ISBN 9789490800376
www.artpapereditions.org
First edition of 500 copies

Between August and November 2014 Stephanie Kiwitt was commissioned by Team Flemish Government Architect to make a photographic work about the outskirts of Brussels: Diegem, Haren, Zaventem, Sint-Stevens-Woluwe, Kraainem, Sint-Pieters-Woluwe, Oudergem, Ukkel, Vorst, Drogenbos, Ruisbroek, Sint-Pieters-Leeuw, Anderlecht, Dilbeek, Groot-Bijgaarden, Sint-Agatha-Berchem, Ganshoren, Jette, Strombeek-Bever, Grimbergen and Vilvoorde.

Text: Steven Humblet
Translation Dutch - English: Gregory Ball
Graphic design: Stephanie Kiwitt
& Jurgen Maelfeyt
Printing: Die Keure, Bruges
Distribution: Idea Books, www.ideabooks.nl

The artist would like to thank Winfried Heininger, Julie Mabilde, Hana Miletić, Peter Swinnen and Joris Vermeir.

This project was initiated and supported by Team Vlaams Bouwmeester.

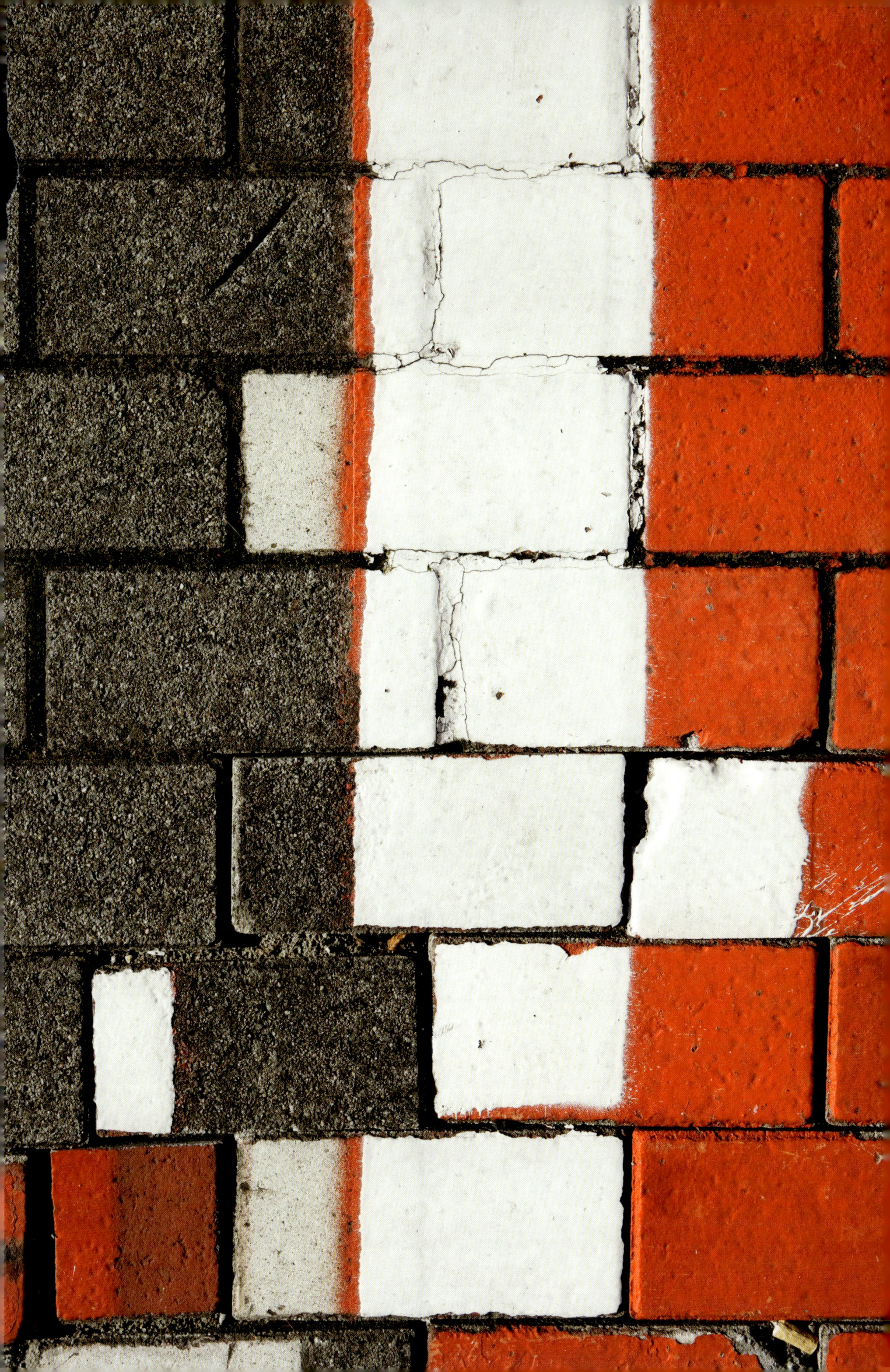

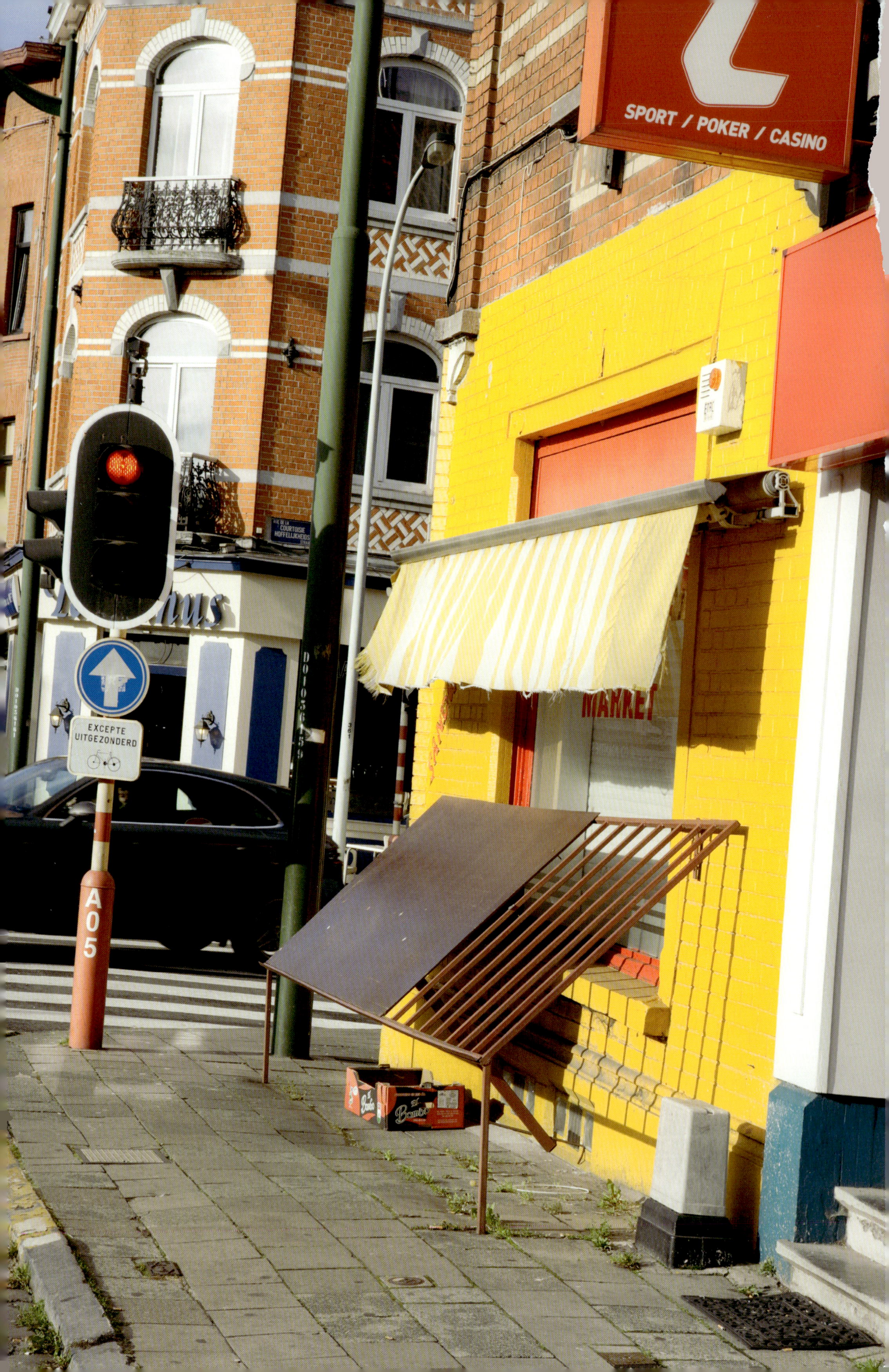
SPORT / POKER / CASINO
EXCEPTE
UITGEZONDERD
A05
MARKET